Strategies to Improve Your Overall Well-Being

A self-help journal for relationships and mental health

Dr. April Givens, PhD

Dr. April Givens Publishing

Texas

Copyright © 2022 Dr. April Givens

All rights reserved. No part of this book may be reproduced or used in any manner without the prior written permission of the copyright owner,
except for the use of brief quotations in a book review.

To request permissions, contact the publisher at
draprilgivensphd@gmail.com.

Paperback: ISBN:9798218061852

First paperback edition October 2022.

Dr. April Givens Publishing

Dallas, TX 75243

How To Use This Journal?

This is a journal of self-reflection and tools you can use to improve your well-being. Please use the space at the bottom of each page to journal your thoughts

Tips to Maintain Your Mental Health As A Mom:

- Acknowledge that your mental health matters.
- Know the signs of a mental health issue.
- Invest in your self-care.
- Keep a daily gratitude journal.
- Cut down on chores and errands.
- Engage in positive self-talk.
- Learn to say no, or at least maybe.
- Maintain healthy habits, such as getting enough. sleep, nutrition, and exercise.
- Know your resources and have a plan to get help.

Abundance Affirmations To Transform Your Mindset:

- I am a magnet for success and good fortune.
- I allow all good things to come into my life.
- I am thankful for all that I have in my life.
- The source of my prosperity is within me.
- I am attracting endless abundance through my gratitude.
- I can feel success coming, and I am ready to welcome it.
- I already have everything I need to create the life I love.
- Abundance in this universe is unlimited, and I will harness the power to receive it.
- I cherish the abundance of happiness that each day brings me.

Affirmations to Help You Overcome Self-Doubt:

- I choose happiness over fear.
- I believe that good things are possible for me.
- There are no limitations to what I can accomplish.
- I deserve complete and unconditional love.
- I don't have to compare myself to other people.
- I deserve to refuel my body and care for myself.
- I won't allow the actions or words of others to define how I view myself.
- I'm confident in my knowledge and understanding of things.

Healing Affirmations To Help You Achieve Inner Peace:

- I allow myself time and space for my soul to heal.
- I attract people who can help me heal through love.
- I choose my body, heart, and soul to heal every day.
- I feel, with every breath I take, a sense of peace and love.
- I see every situation as an opportunity to heal and grow.
- I'm inhaling strength with every breath I take and exhaling my fear.
- I manifest perfect health by letting go of what doesn't serve me.
- I am a channel of peace and well-being, and my need for peace is abundantly met.

How Can You Restore Your Mental Energy:

- Practice gratitude daily.
- Do things that make you feel positive.
- Rethink the way you expend your energy.
- Keep your to-do list simple and realistic.
- Spending some time practicing meditation each day.
- Say yes to self-acceptance and self-care always.
- Do at least one thing every day that makes you feel genuinely happy.
- Take care of your physical self, by eating healthy, taking adequate sleep, caring about your hygiene, exercising regularly.

Positive Affirmations That'll Change The Way You Think:

- I live in the present with confidence for the future.
- Every experience in my life helps me to grow.
- I radiate love, happiness, grace, and positivity.
- I am forgiving. My compassion replaces anger with love.
- I quickly find solutions to challenges and move past them.
- I attract positive circumstances and positive people.
- I am grateful for this moment, and I see the joy in it.
- I am courageous and overcome my fears by confronting them.
- Everything happens for a reason. Everything leads to something positive.

Positive Affirmations To Boost Your Confidence:

- I am becoming a better version of myself one day at a time.
- I believe in my abilities and express my true self with ease.
- As I take on new challenges I feel calm, confident, and powerful.
- I will be open-minded and always eager to explore new avenues to success.
- The universe is filled with endless opportunities for my career.
- I can let go of old, negative beliefs that have stood in the way of my success.
- I am valuable and will make powerful contributions to the world today.
- My ability to conquer challenges is limitless; my potential to succeed is infinite.
- I am surrounded by supportive, positive people who believe in me and want to see me succeed.

Ways You Can Prioritize Your Mental Health:

- Start a gratitude journal to express yourself.
- Always treat yourself with kindness and respect.
- Surround yourself with people that bring you positive energy.
- Practice meditation and yoga to create mental clarity and calmness.
- Stay physically active, make healthy food choices and get enough sleep.
- Take part in activities that challenge your creativity and make you feel productive.
- If you notice that your mental health is hurting your daily life, you may benefit from speaking to a mental health professional.

Ways To Become A Better Person:

- Consider your impact on others.
- Think before you speak.
- Practice random acts of kindness.
- Let go of anger.
- Use your strengths.
- Recognize your weaknesses.
- Follow through on your commitments.
- Practice compassion.

Symptoms Of Borderline Personality Disorder:

- Intense fear of abandonment.
- Impulsive, self-destructive behaviors.
- Ongoing feelings of emptiness.
- A pattern of unstable intense relationships.
- Rapid changes in self-identity and self-image.
- Feeling suspicious or out of touch with reality.
- Periods of stress-related paranoia and loss of contact with reality.
- Wide mood swings lasting from a few hours to a few days.

Affirmations You Can Use To Overcome Social Anxiety:

- I am free from societal judgments.
- I am happy with who I am.
- I can stay calm around other people.
- I trust in the infinite abilities of my higher self.
- I am confident in my public speaking skills.
- The people I spend my time with like me as a person.
- I am able to make positive connections with others.
- I handle social situations with ease and confidence.
- I am grateful for all the good people in my life.
- I welcome new friends into my life, and they welcome me warmly as well.

Affirmations For Anxiety Relief:

- I choose to fill my mind with positive, nurturing, and healing thoughts.
- I harness the surplus of energy I have and focus it on my goals.
- Living in a state of curiosity and child-like wonder brings me peace of mind.
- Each exhalation I take calms my nerves and brings ease to my body and mind.
- With each new breath, I inhale strength and exhale fear. I am learning that it is safe for me to heal and grow.

Affirmations To Increase Your Positive Self-Talk:

- I am happy and satisfied with my life.
- I expect good results, good health, and happiness.
- I let go of the past and expect a wonderful future.
- Every day, I am improving my life.
- I always expect constructive and productive results.
- Today I put my full trust in my inner guidance.
- I will grow in strength with every forward step I take.
- I let go of worries and fears that drain my energy and waste my time.
- I surround myself with people who like me and treat me well.

Anger Management Strategies
To Help You Calm Down:

- Learn to pay attention to what triggers your anger and you'll get better at recognizing the warning signs.
- One of the best things you can do when your anger is rising is to remove yourself from the situation.
- Taking deep breaths can help you relax your muscles and also calms down your nerves.
- Talking through an issue or expressing your feelings to a friend or a family member may be helpful.
- Practicing regular exercise also helps you decompress, reduce stress, which might help improve your frustration tolerance.
- Reframe your thoughts when you find yourself thinking about things that fuel your anger.

Affirmations To Help You Set Boundaries With Love:

- I am guided by thoughts of love and kindness.
- I am free to speak my truth: clearly and with love.
- I do not need to agree with someone in order to love them.
- I welcome positive and uplifting vibrations into my space.
- I can respect the feelings of others and still honor my own.
- I am free to leave relationships that aren't healthy for me, or that don't nourish my soul.
- I free myself of all emotions that are not mine to carry and I willingly give them back to their source.
- My love is a precious gift that I have the power to choose when, how, and to whom to give.

Bad Habits You Must Break To Improve Your Mental Health:

- You're not exercising.
- You won't let go of guilt.
- You don't pay attention to your posture.
- You hold onto toxic relationships.
- You're a people pleaser.
- You're always codependent on others.
- You keep on self-sabotaging yourself.
- You compare yourself to others.
- You don't have a healthy sleep schedule.
- You keep letting stress get the best of you.

Bad Habits You Must Break To Heal Your Anxiety:

- Not following a healthy diet.
- Not maintaining a work-life balance.
- Not staying connected with friends and loved ones.
- Bad exercise habits that affect your mental health include exercising irregularly or not at all, exercising to the point of exhaustion, practicing bad form, and engaging in only one form of exercise.
- Sleeping too little or too much has a significant effect on your health and mental well-being.
- Isolation or lack of connection for a longer period of time can lead to chronic health problems, as well as anxiety, depression, and feelings of loneliness.

Bad Habits That Interfere With Your Mental Health:

- You miss out on sleep.
- You don't exercise.
- You keep toxic relationships.
- You don't talk to anyone.
- You let anger stay around.
- You keep searching for perfectionism.
- You always have to please everyone.
- You keep letting stress get the best of you.
- You compare yourself negatively to others.

Benefits Of Gratitude You Should Know About:

- Gratitude can help relieve stress.
- Strengthens your social relationships.
- Gratitude can help you sleep better.
- Helps enhance empathy and reduce aggression.
- Gratitude improves physical health.
- Strengthens your immune system.
- Helps you accomplish more goals.
- Gratitude can increase your self-esteem.
- Gratitude can make you feel more positive emotions.

Benefits Of Paying More Attention To Your Feelings:

- You'll learn to trust yourself more.
- You'll be less vulnerable to what other people think.
- You'll be able to connect with other people better.
- Paying attention encourages you to feel more positive feelings, and reduce your negative feelings.
- You'll be more present in your body and in the moment.
- Paying attention helps you do better in your life.
- Paying attention can help you focus your awareness on a particular aspect of your environment and in important decisions of your life.

Benefits of Living Consciously You Should Know:

- Increased self-awareness.
- Having enhanced mental clarity.
- Enhanced problem-solving skills.
- Being aware of your strengths and weaknesses.
- Developing the ability to control your emotional state.
- Developing better relationships with other people.
- Being able to develop conscious eating, exercise, and health habits.
- Being able to consciously control your thoughts and the ability to discipline your mind.

Coping Strategies You Can Use For Social Anxiety:

- Avoid using negative coping strategies.
- Explore specific situations that trigger anxiety.
- Learn to acknowledge and set aside your distracting and disturbing thoughts.
- Simple breathing exercises will help you stay calm.
- Visualization exercises and journaling can also be helpful.
- Actively look for supportive social environments that can help you overcome your fears.
- Ask yourself questions to challenge your negative thoughts.
- Perform small acts of kindness which can help reduce the desire to avoid social situations.

Daily Habits That Can Actually Change Your Life:

- Drinking a glass of water when you wake up.
- Establishing a meaningful morning ritual.
- Surrounding yourself with positive people.
- Maintaining proper hygiene every day.
- Creating the habit of being punctual.
- Exercising for at least fifteen minutes every day.
- Prioritizing sleep and developing a sleeping ritual.
- Practice thinking about the things you have to be thankful for.
- Training yourself to eat a balanced and healthy diet.
- Appreciating yourself for the things you have done so far.

Dating Boundaries May Sound Like:

- Clarifying your communication styles.
- Taking responsibility for your choices.
- Respecting each other's expectations.
- Saying no without feeling bad.
- Breaking the stigma around personal space.
- Not leaving things open-ended.
- Being clear about commitment and what you want.
- Asking your partner what they are feeling versus guessing.

Energy-Draining Everyday Habits You Should Avoid:

- Being in a negative environment.
- Complaining about things without changing them.
- Constantly worrying about unnecessary things.
- Having processed, unhealthy foods and not eating healthy.
- Using social media not to make yourself feel bad. Comparing other people's lives with yourself without realizing they are at a different stage than yours.
- Sleeping too much does not increase your energy, create energy reserves or make you more present.
- Not taking things personally will save you a lot of stress and your workplace a lot of needless strain.

Essential Life Truths You Need To Live By:

- Don't wait for the perfect moment; Start before you feel ready.
- Do what you can to take care of your body.
- Spend more time looking for a solution than dwelling on the problem.
- Success does not bring happiness, happiness brings it.
- The more you give thanks, the more good things flow to you.
- Your worth is not dependent on whether you have a career, partner, beautiful figure, or home.
- If you have the courage to get through the situation you fear, you will look back and realize there was nothing to be afraid of -- it was all an illusion.

Examples of Non-Negotiables In A Relationship:

- You miss out on sleep.
- You don't exercise.
- You keep toxic relationships.
- You don't talk to anyone.
- You let anger stay around.
- You keep searching for perfectionism.
- You always have to please everyone.
- You keep letting stress get the best of you.
- You compare yourself negatively to others.

Exciting Reasons You Should Smile Every Day:

- Smiling can help you fight illness.
- You can become more creative.
- People will trust you more.
- Smiling boosts your productivity.
- Smiling can help increase your lifespan.
- It makes you look more attractive.
- It makes you look more successful.
- Smiling makes you a more positive person.
- Smiling de-stresses your even days in advance.

Friendship Green Flags
You Should Know About:

- You can be yourself with them.
- You take care of each other.
- They accept you as the person that you are.
- They're eager to defend you or protect you.
- You also feel like what you're communicating is being heard. They are taking time to listen and understand your point of view.
- They want to help you to be a better person, encouraging you to follow your dreams.
- The friends who try to uplift you and motivate you to reach greater heights are precious.

Gaslighting Signs May Look Like:

- You are questioning your thoughts.
- You have trouble making simple decisions.
- Always thinking it's your fault when things go wrong.
- You feel as though you're a much weaker version of yourself.
- You feel misunderstood, hopeless, and depressed.
- You are afraid of speaking up or expressing your emotions.
- You feel like you're constantly overreacting or are "too sensitive."
- You are being more anxious and less confident than you used to be.

Gentle Reminders

- Recognize self-sabotaging habits.
- Identify root causes of the behavior.
- Take time for self-reflection.
- Find your inner positive voice.
- Change your pattern of behavior.
- Allow yourself to notice without judgment.
- Stay compassionate towards yourself.
- Practice self-acceptance and self-care.
- Use strategies to help you manage avoidance and procrastination.

Harsh Life Truths That Will Make You a Strong Person:

- Everyone puts their own interests first.
- Your actions define you, not your thoughts.
- You're not everyone's cup of tea–and that's OK.
- We can't control the past, and wasting time to worry about it is lost time. It is the most valuable thing you can spend.
- Experiencing loss is something we will all have to go through at some point in our lives.
- Our words have the power to hurt, shame, and oppress. Our arguments with others are pointless. Use your words carefully.
- Your most difficult moments are good lessons you couldn't have learned any other way.
- Start living a purposeful life and try to mend broken relationships, because you never know when life will end.

Harsh Truths About Life You Should Know:

- Life will never be perfect.
- You have more time than you think you do.
- Self-respect leads to universal respect.
- Don't let anyone set your boundaries.
- Do what you love, love what you do.
- Nothing lasts forever–and that's a good thing.
- Many things you can't choose, but you have a choice in everything you do.
- You can't control a lot of things–but you can control how you respond.

Healing Affirmations To Help You Achieve Inner Peace:

- I allow myself time and space for my soul to heal.
- I attract people who can help me heal through love.
- I choose my body, heart, and soul to heal every day.
- I feel, with every breath I take, a sense of peace and love.
- I see every situation as an opportunity to heal and grow.
- I'm inhaling strength with every breath I take and exhaling my fear.
- I manifest perfect health by letting go of what doesn't serve me.
- I am a channel of peace and well-being, and my need for peace is abundantly met.

Healthy Morning Habits To Start Your Day Right:

- Get some natural light right away.
- Set and affirm your goals for the day.
- Exercise your body and brain.
- Eat a nutritious and balanced breakfast.
- Ask yourself: What are you grateful for?
- Do something fun or creative.
- Write or review your daily to-do list.

Healthy Ways to Deal With Worry:

- Change your perspective.
- Face your worries.
- Accept the things you cannot change.
- Spend more time in the present moment.
- Don't try to guess what's on someone's mind.
- Turn your negative thoughts around.
- Keep a daily emotions journal.
- Maintain a regular sleep schedule.
- Determine whether some of your worries are simply noise.
- Give yourself time to relax daily and practice mindfulness.

How Can You Brighten Up Someone's Day:

- **Practice acts of kindness.**
- **Listen to someone else's problems.**
- **Make a meal for someone who's stressed.**
- **Give someone even a stranger a genuine compliment.**
- **Give someone your time, just listen without judgment.**
- **Ask elderly people in your neighborhood if they need anything at the store when you're out anyway.**
- **Offer to help an overwhelmed friend or co-worker.**
- **Reach out to call a friend, family member, or neighbor who is experiencing loneliness or isolation and needs help.**

How Can You Manage Self-Sabotaging Behaviors:

- Recognize self-sabotaging habits.
- Identify root causes of the behavior.
- Take time for self-reflection.
- Find your inner positive voice.
- Change your pattern of behavior.
- Allow yourself to notice without judgment.
- Stay compassionate towards yourself.
- Practice self-acceptance and self-care.
- Use strategies to help you manage avoidance and procrastination.

How Can You Restore Your Mental Energy:

- Practice gratitude daily.
- Do things that make you feel positive.
- Rethink the way you expend your energy.
- Keep your to-do list simple and realistic.
- Spending some time practicing meditation each day.
- Say yes to self-acceptance and self-care always.
- Do at least one thing every day that makes you feel genuinely happy.
- Take care of your physical self, by eating healthy, taking adequate sleep, caring about your hygiene, exercising regularly.

How Can You Set Boundaries With Your Parents:

- Be clear and concise with them.
- Be assertive and compassionate with them.
- Release any guilt about having boundaries.
- Don't let your emotions get the best of you.
- Set a limit from a calm, respectful, emotion-neutral space.
- Give your parents the benefit of the doubt, and talk to them.
- Frame your boundaries with gratitude and appreciation.
- Remember, boundaries should be healthy for everyone involved.
- Be respectful of boundaries that they may then set with you.

How Can You Spend Your Mental Health Day:

- **Practice self-compassion and positive self-talk.**
- **Listen to music that improves your mood, or a podcast that inspires you.**
- **Practice good hygiene or pampering yourself with a facial or a massage.**
- **Take some time out for yourself to indulge in your creative passions.**
- **Set yourself up for a good night's sleep - try getting 7-8 hours as a minimum.**
- **Plan time off work - be it a trip away, or simply enjoying time at home to relax.**
- **Spend time with your partner, friends, or family, whether that's virtually or in-person.**

How Can You Stop Procrastinating:

- Get organized with your work.
- Set simple and achievable goals.
- After you set your goals, create a timeline to complete them.
- Set a proper deadline for your goals.
- Reflect on the root causes of procrastination.
- Rid yourself of all potential disruptions before you begin working.
- Get an accountability partner to hold you accountable, motivate you, and inspire you to overcome procrastination.

How Can You Support Your Friends If They Are Struggling:

- Listen and don't panic in front of them.
- Acknowledge that what's happening must be difficult.
- Make sure that they are still eating, sleeping, and staying hydrated, and encourage other helpful things such as taking time away from social media and writing down how they feel.
- Make sure that your friend knows that they are not alone and they don't have to deal with this on their own.
- Encourage your friend to do the things that will make them feel better, and remind them of the importance of self-care.
- Help your friend to make an appointment, and remind them that the professional can help them and that it's better to reach out for that help now before things get worse.

How To Deal With The Grieving Process:

- You may feel broken in grief.
- There is no specific timeline to be done grieving.
- Feeling sad, frightened, or lonely is a normal reaction to loss.
- It's important to appreciate the small wins while you are grieving.
- Understand that your grieving process will be unique to you.
- What other people think about your grief is none of your business.
- Accept that grief can trigger many different and unexpected emotions.
- You don't have to suffer, find a supportive community or therapist.

How Can You Tell If Your Inner Child Is Wounded:

- You have trouble dealing with boundaries.
- You're scared to speak up to advocate for or defend yourself.
- You have problems sustaining healthy and respectful relationships.
- You learned to avoid or repress your emotions as they were associated with feelings of neglect from your childhood.
- You will do anything not to lose anyone and strive to be a "people pleaser."
- You may have difficulty controlling your emotions, and frequently feel guilty when you feel a "negative" emotion like anger or sadness.

How To Give Yourself The Validation You Crave:

- Be present with your emotions.
- Notice how you feel and what you need.
- Accept your feelings and needs without any judgment.
- Reflect on the ways you feel the emotion in your body.
- Consider the actions that go with the emotion.
- Surround yourself with positive people.
- Get in the habit of asking yourself, "What do I need right now?"
- Always remember, practice is an important part of learning self-validation!

How Toxic Relationships Affect Your Mental Health:

- Toxic relationships create mental strain and stress.
- Negativity becomes part of your everyday life.
- Negative emotions are capable of tearing down your more healthy habits.
- Being treated poorly leads to a poor relationship with yourself.
- Unstable relationships with family members and close friends can contribute to depression.
- Negative relationships can lead to or worsen anxiety and stress disorders.
- Toxic relationships can isolate you from other more empowering & supportive relationships.

How To Help Someone Cope With Fear of Abandonment:

- Start the conversation. Encourage them to talk about it.
- Assure them that you won't abandon them.
- Learn to have difficult conversations in calm, respectful ways.
- People with abandonment issues may benefit from self-care.
- Avoid pushing for answers, and allow the person to open up in their own time.
- Whether it makes sense to you or not, understand that the fear is real for them.
- Seek out the help of a mental health professional, such as a therapist or counselor.

Men's Mental Health Tips All Dads Can Adopt:

- Go easy on yourself.
- When stress is getting the better of you, pause.
- Take good care of yourself.
- Take 30 minutes for yourself each day.
- Prioritize sleep and make time for exercise.
- Practice mindfulness, thinking about what you're grateful for, and setting your intentions.
- Talk with other dads about their early experiences as a father and take tips from them.
- Put the work in to keep relationships going with your friends, family, and partner.
- Reach out for help when required.

Mental Benefits of Exercising You Should Know About:

- Exercising helps to improve the body's overall ability to respond to stress.
- Helps increase self-esteem and self-confidence.
- Prevents cognitive decline and memory loss by strengthening the part of the brain responsible for memory and learning.
- Even just moderate exercise throughout the week can improve depression and anxiety.
- Exercising can help you build resilience and cope in a healthy way, instead of resorting to negative behaviors.
- Exercise also helps regulate your circadian rhythm, our bodies' built-in alarm clock that controls when we feel tired and when we feel alert.

Morning Routine Tips That Support Mental Health:

- Choose a softer alarm sound to wake up.
- Start your day by drinking water.
- Eat a healthy and nourishing breakfast.
- Listen to relaxing music or do guided meditation.
- Practice gratitude and recite morning affirmations.
- Avoid checking your phone first thing in the morning.
- Take some deep breaths to get into a relaxed state.
- Take a walk outdoors, it is a calming and grounding way to begin your day.
- Exercise in the morning to improve your focus and energy for the rest of the day.

Mental Health Tips For Men

When Things Get Tough:

- Be honest about how you are feeling.
- Embrace and accept who you are.
- Try to integrate healthier eating patterns and fulfilling nutritious meals into your diet.
- Take some time for yourself, creating off time to relax, focus on yourself and unwind.
- Include some form of exercise in your daily routine to help you feel relaxed as well as keep physically fit.
- Getting proper rest every day is important as worsening mental health conditions are extremely common amongst individuals facing sleep problems.
- Reach out for professional help or start talking to your loved ones when you need help.

Methods You Can Use To Declutter Your Mental Space:

- Be present in the moment.
- Declutter your physical environment.
- Do more of what makes you happy.
- Practice mindfulness through meditation.
- Taking regular daily walks can also help clear your mind.
- Limit the amount of information coming in.
- Try putting your thoughts down in writing so you can more easily explore them.
- Go through your past and discard memories that are not serving you.

Myths About Mental Health You Should Know About:

- Mental health problems are uncommon.
- Mental health problems are purely biological or genetic.
- Mental health disorders are often life-long and difficult to treat.
- Individuals who experience mental health symptoms will never recover.
- Everyone who has a mental illness needs medication to manage symptoms.
- Individuals who experience mental health symptoms will never recover.
- Someone living with a mental illness is more likely to commit a crime or be violent.

Nighttime Routine Tips You Can Use For Your Well-Being:

- Schedule technology-free time before bed.
- Regular exercise can improve sleep, but you're better off saving intense workouts for morning or afternoon.
- Relaxation techniques such as progressive muscle relaxation often help improve sleep.
- Practicing mindfulness meditation, in particular, may help improve your ability to release the day's stress and tension in preparation for a good night's sleep.
- A cup of herbal & a good book is probably a good way to wind down before bed and also a great way to practice self-care.
- Playing soft, soothing music as you prepare for bed can trigger the release of hormones that help improve your mood.

Physical Self-Care Looks Like:

- **Doing breathing exercises.**
- **Maintaining a healthy diet.**
- **Developing a regular sleep routine.**
- **Exercise is good for your mental health.**
- **Playing a sport you enjoy, or take a yoga class.**
- **Allowing your body to rest and recover.**

Positive Affirmations For Stress Relief:

- I release all tension from my mind and body.
- I prioritize the things that make me feel calm.
- I am capable of getting through tough times.
- I see challenges where others see difficulties.
- My true purpose has no time limit and no deadline.
- I trust the Universe is looking out for my higher good.
- I choose to respond to situations from a place of peace.
- Calmness washes over me with every deep breath I take.

Positive Affirmations That Can Change Your Life:

- Every morning I wake up with thoughts and feelings that are nourishing.
- My thoughts are filled with positivity and my life is plentiful with prosperity.
- I radiate love and others reflect love back to me.
- I am talented. I have been gifted with endless skills that I hone each day.
- My efforts are being supported by the universe; my dreams manifest into reality before my eyes.
- I forgive those who have harmed me in my past and peacefully detach from them.
- My future is an ideal projection of what I envision now.

Positive Affirmations To Heal Childhood Trauma:

- I am safe at this moment.
- I am a likable and lovable person.
- I am a valid human being with feelings and needs.
- I deserve to be respected and treated with love.
- Boundary setting helps me to create safety within my life.
- I do not blame myself for my childhood experiences/trauma.
- I choose to create an atmosphere of peace and safety.
- My abuse/traumatic experiences do not define who I am as a person.
- I am changing in positive ways. I am making peace with my past and accepting myself.

Positive Affirmations To Help Heal Your Broken Heart:

- I have power over my own life.
- There is something better waiting for me.
- I am learning to love myself unconditionally.
- I choose to release anger, hurt, and negative self-talk.
- Each day in every way I am peaceful, healed, and happy.
- I am grateful for everything I learned in my last relationship.
- I find strength through my struggle and trust my greatness.
- Love is my guide in all of my relationships. I am healed and whole.
- I am grateful for having loved and for the lessons I have learned.

Positive Affirmations To Help Kick Start Your Week:

- I am exactly where I need to be.
- I am getting better and better every day.
- I am not pushed by my problems; I am led by my dreams.
- I do not waste away a single day of my life. I get every ounce of value out of each of my days on this planet—today, tomorrow, and every day.
- I accept myself for who I am and create peace, power, and confidence of mind and of heart.
- I'm capable of overcoming any hurdles that come at me.
- I am having a positive and inspiring impact on the people I come into contact with.
- I choose to learn and grow every day, no matter what work or life throws at me.

Powerful Life Lessons Everyone Should Learn:

- If you don't believe in yourself, nobody will.
- Hard work always pays. Never ever give up your dreams
- Learn something new every day. Make everyday count
- Gain confidence. Make your presence noticed.
- Love yourself and others will love you also.
- The world won't change if you don't change.
- Life is all about the journey and less about the destination.
- Honesty is the best policy because no matter how good you are at telling lies, the truth will always come out.
- Your family and friends are the best you got. Preserve them with all your heart.

Powerful Reasons You Should Express Yourself:

- You start to develop stronger boundaries.
- It helps you to be more confident.
- You experience a boost of creativity.
- It helps you practice acceptance.
- You can improve your communication skills.
- You can enhance relationships with yourself and others.
- It gives you a glimpse of what is in your heart and mind.
- You can conquer your fear and soothe your anxiety.
- You can improve your well-being by expressing yourself.

Powerful Tips To Overcome Negative Thoughts:

- Practice positive affirmations.
- Pay attention to the thought itself.
- Imagine a stop sign literally.
- Learn to cope with criticism.
- Surround yourself with positive people.
- Write your negative thoughts down.
- List five things that you are grateful for right now.
- Practice being mindful and engage in regular exercise.
- Counter negative thoughts with uplifting visualizations.
- Reframe your thoughts and focus on the positive.

Practical Ways To Start Working On Self-Improvement:

- Practice positive self-talk.
- Incorporate gratitude into your daily life.
- Learn visualization techniques.
- Practice daily mindfulness.
- Forgive yourself and others.
- Start being kind to yourself.
- Surround yourself with positive people.
- Align your priorities with your goals and values.
- Try to get seven to eight hours of sleep each night.
- Take time to connect with others, and have some relaxation or downtime for yourself.

Reasons Why Listening Is Important In Our Life:

- Listening helps build trust.
- Listening encourages empathy around people.
- Listening enhances your ability to understand better and makes you a better communicator.
- It helps an individual to develop a better understanding of its social and professional environment.
- Listening can help eliminate conflict, anger, and resentment.
- Listening helps in recognizing others' perspectives and feelings and helps us appreciate them.
- Learning to really listen to what people say can help you identify signs of early onset of mental health concerns.

Reasons Why You Should Express Gratitude Everyday:

- Gratitude helps you to reach your goals.
- Gratitude benefits physical health.
- Gratitude can improve your relationships.
- It helps to preserve precious memories.
- Gratitude makes you a happier person.
- Gratitude improves your communication skills.
- It promotes better sleep quality and relaxation.
- Gratitude can improve productivity and performance.
- It can help you cope with stress and boost your mental strength.

Reasons You Should Stop Comparing Yourself To Others:

- Nobody is perfect.
- Comparing yourself limits self-awareness.
- Comparing yourself lowers your self-esteem.
- Comparing yourself makes you feel inferior.
- It doesn't help you accomplish your goals.
- Comparing yourself is an unproductive waste of time.
- Comparing yourself distracts you from improving yourself.
- Comparing yourself to others will make you feel depressed.
- Comparing is dangerous to your mental health.

Red Flags In A Relationship You Shouldn't Ignore:

- The relationship is all about them.
- They call you names in arguments.
- They threaten to break up with you all the time.
- They make you feel personally responsible and guilty for all their misfortunes.
- They may make you choose them over significant others as an expression of "love".
- They demand your phone, email, and social media passwords.
- Any form of abuse, from the seemingly mild to the overtly obvious—verbal, emotional, psychological, and certainly physical abuse is a major red flag.

Red Flags of Gaslighting In A Relationship:

- Their actions do not match their words.
- They try to align people against you.
- They project their problems onto you
- They control your 'other' relationships.
- They never let you talk during a conflict.
- They do not respect your boundaries.
- Your anxieties and insecurities have increased.
- They accuse you of being "too sensitive," "hysterical," or "overly emotional".
- They attack the people, things, and values that are most dear to you.

Reframing Your Thoughts
To Have Positive Feelings:

- Identify automatic thoughts and replace them with positive thoughts.
- Every time you're feeling anxious take out your thoughts and emotions for a second and think about what the facts of the situation are.
- Write down your thoughts and take that list of specific negative thoughts you wrote down and change the wording.
- Repeating your positive thought over and over to yourself, out loud, and even sharing them with others.
- Talk to yourself the way you would talk to your friend.
- Transform your internal negative dialogue into positive.
- Practice gratitude daily, as your mindset can shift from being negative to being more positive.

How To Relax Your Mind and Body From Anxiety:

- Slow, deep breathing techniques where you focus on breathing in and out can help you relax.
- Taking a walk or doing some physical activity can help clear your mind.
- Making time to do things you enjoy can also help you relax. You can indulge in your hobbies.
- Smelling something pleasant, lighting a candle, or using a diffuser with a calming essential oil.
- Practicing mindfulness can help you stay present and you can create a calm state of mind when you feel your thoughts racing and anxiety building.
- If your anxiety is making it hard to function, talking to someone you trust can help.

How Can You Restore Your Mental Energy:

- Practice gratitude daily.
- Do things that make you feel positive.
- Rethink the way you expend your energy.
- Keep your to-do list simple and realistic.
- Spending some time practicing meditation each day.
- Say yes to self-acceptance and self-care always.
- Do at least one thing every day that makes you feel genuinely happy.
- Take care of your physical self, by eating healthy, taking adequate sleep, caring about your hygiene, exercising regularly.

Remember This When You're Feeling Overwhelmed:

- Remember that feeling overwhelmed is OK.
- When you're feeling overwhelmed, your life isn't falling apart—your thoughts are.
- Feeling overwhelmed is your mind's way of telling you to slow down if you want to live a healthier life.
- When you feel overwhelmed, try to focus on reframing the experience and see it from a different angle.
- Writing down why you feel overwhelmed is another great way to help alleviate those feelings.
- You can use breathing techniques to have a soothing effect on your system when you're feeling overwhelmed.
- You can reach out to a friend for a chat or pick up the phone and call a family member.

Revealing Signs Of Self-Sabotaging Behavior:

- You procrastinate on important tasks.
- You have a lack of commitment.
- You have a lack of consistency.
- You are constantly seeking validation.
- You are constantly comparing yourself to others.
- You are intensely fearful and full of criticism.
- You are always trying to control everything.
- You limit your happiness to materialistic things.
- You refuse to seek help when you need it.

Self-Care Ideas To Help You Through A Bad Day:

- Go for a long walk in nature.
- Journal about how you're feeling.
- Exercise in a way that feels good for you.
- Write down 5 things you're grateful for.
- Call or text someone you love.
- Cook or order your favorite meal.
- Write down 5 things you love about yourself.
- Just sit outside and breathe the fresh air.
- Step outside in nature and grab some vitamin D.
- Make a list of the people and things you are thankful for.
- Remind yourself of the good that exists all around you.

Self-Care Tips For Managing Loneliness:

- Acknowledge your feelings of loneliness.
- Know when to engage or disengage from the online world when combating loneliness.
- Practice self-compassion and positive self-talk.
- Take yourself on a date. Self-dates can be a powerful tool for learning how to be happy alone.
- Practice good hygiene or pamper yourself with a facial or a massage.
- Take some time out for yourself to indulge in your creative passions.
- You can volunteer in person or help out remotely from home. Either way, helping others can make you feel good. This can help you feel connected to others while still getting in some quality alone time.

Self-Discipline Benefits And Its Importance In Your Life:

- Self-discipline is a skill that enables you to stick to your decisions and plans until you accomplish them.
- Self-discipline helps you see the value of delayed gratification, which pays off down the line.
- Self-discipline is vital for overcoming eating disorders, addictions, smoking, drinking, and other negative habits.
- It enables you to stay in control of yourself and of your reaction to any situation.
- It is also an important requirement for studying and learning, for developing any skill, and for success in self-improvement, spiritual growth, and meditation.
- Improve your relationships because you become a person who follows through on your commitments.

Self-Growth Journey Looks Like:

- **Improving your self-awareness.**
- **Knowing and building your identity.**
- **Discovering and developing your talents.**
- **Reframing your failures.**
- **Being grateful for what you have.**
- **Setting attainable goals for yourself.**
- **Not giving up in difficult times.**
- **Reaching your true potential.**

Self-Love Habits Every *Person Should Adopt:*

- Stop comparing yourself to others.
- Don't be afraid to let go of toxic people.
- Speak kindly to yourself, and don't call yourself mean things.
- Trust yourself to make good decisions for yourself.
- Take action, and know that your voice is just as important as anyone else's.
- Practicing meditation to stay present and mindful.
- Exercising and having a proper sleep schedule on a regular basis keeps your body strong and improves your health.
- Find some self-love affirmations that connect with you and repeat them every day.

Self-Reflective Questions You Should Ask Yourself:

- What's the most spontaneous thing you've ever done?
- Which have been your best moments in life so far?
- If you could turn back time, what would you do differently?
- Which three things are more important to you than anything else in your life?
- What advice or encouragement would you give to your future self?
- If you could only use five words, how would you describe yourself?
- What one thing have you wanted to do but not yet been brave enough to try?

Signs Of An Emotionally Unavailable Partner:

- They never make an effort.
- They don't like making plans.
- They don't respect your time.
- They avoid the word 'relationship'.
- They show up late or blow off plans.
- They're not comfortable with your emotions.
- They don't put the same effort into the relationship.
- They choose physical intimacy over emotional intimacy.

Signs That Stress Is Affecting *Your Relationship:*

- You're taking your stress out on each other.
- You may become less empathetic to your partner.
- You mistakenly think you're falling out of love.
- Your intimacy has diminished or is non-existent.
- You feel hopeless about your relationship.
- You are continuously having arguments and disagreements with your partner.
- You tend to say the wrong things at the wrong time, which can result in someone else being hurt.
- You face more conflict and communication issues, and your partner is left feeling disconnected and hopeless, threatening their mental state as well.

Signs to Help You Spot Narcissistic Behavior:

- Have an exaggerated sense of self-importance.
- Regularly cross boundaries and break rules.
- Difficulty with attachment and dependency.
- Exaggerated need for attention and validation.
- An inability to communicate or work as part of a team.
- Lacks empathy and doesn't try to identify other's needs.
- Expects special, favorable treatment or compliance with his or her wishes.
- Exploits and takes advantage of others to achieve personal ends.

Signs You Are Growing As A Person:

- Your life is set up on your terms.
- You are always challenging and pushing yourself.
- You are spending less time with people who drain you.
- You are becoming more assertive and learning to say no.
- You realize that rest is an important factor in your journey.
- You have your unique mission in life that only you can do.
- You remember all the things you truly love, uninfluenced by any outside sources.
- You have begun to understand yourself better and aren't afraid to express your interests to others.

Signs You Could Be Emotionally Numb:

- You cannot express strong negative or positive emotions.
- You frequently question the meaning or purpose of your life.
- You have a lack of interest in activities others find enjoyable
- You have suicidal thoughts that seem to come out of really nowhere.
- Your emotions are only felt in the body as sensations, but not by the mind
- The lack of connection to your feelings does set you apart. You may feel like other people are living a more vivid life than you are.

Simple Habits That Can Change Your Life:

- **Creating a morning routine.**
- **Setting boundaries.**
- **Exercising and staying healthy.**
- **Maintaining a gratitude journal.**
- **Say "no" when you mean no.**
- **Learning something new every day.**
- **Organize to-do lists based on life goals.**
- **Remove toxic friendships.**

Signs You Need Emotional Boundaries in Your Life:

- Your energy is always drained.
- You allow negative self-talk.
- You're not prioritizing your needs.
- You don't know how to say "no".
- You give a lot, but don't receive back.
- You take responsibility for other people's thoughts, feelings, make them responsible for yours.
- You allow poor behavior at the expense of your well-being.
- You're often emotionally exhausted after speaking to certain people.

Simple Ways To Train Your Brain For Happiness:

- Ask yourself if you're thinking positively.
- Get a perspective – acknowledge what you have.
- Celebrate your successes, even the small ones.
- Practice mindful listening and let go of worry or stress.
- Create a healthy mindset while you are talking to yourself.
- Give yourself a daily reminder to focus on something you have to be grateful for.
- Prioritize sleep — your mood and immune system are counting on it.
- Spend a few minutes each day writing about something that made you happy.

Steps To Create The Life You Want:

- See yourself how you want to be.
- Adopt the growth mindset.
- Stay focused on what you want in life.
- Take responsibility for your actions.
- Don't let setbacks discourage you.
- Don't worry about other's opinions.
- Refocus when change happens.
- Always be open to new opportunities.

Things To Stop Feeling Guilty For:

- Prioritizing yourself over others.
- Standing up for yourself.
- Giving yourself a break.
- Never feel guilty for saying no.
- Not having time for everyone.
- Making self-care a priority.
- Doing the right thing, even if it hurts someone.
- Distancing yourself from a toxic family member.
- Following your aspirations, not someone else's.

Things You Need To Keep Reminding Yourself Everyday

- Remind yourself that who you are is enough.
- Remind yourself daily that this moment is your life.
- Doing things you love will never be a waste of time.
- Everything worth fighting for is hard to get.
- Remind yourself of the growth you've made.
- The fact that you haven't given up is a success in itself.
- Remind yourself that you always get through.
- In every tough situation, kindness must be attempted first.
- Remind yourself that each day is a new beginning, each morning is a new life.

Ways You Can Overcome Your Insecurities:

- **Identify your insecurities first.**
- **Accept that everything is subjective.**
- **Engage in positive self-talk and use affirmations.**
- **Practicing self-acceptance and fully accept yourself despite your flaws, imperfections, and limitations.**
- **Consider what is meaningful; think about what you want to achieve and how you are going to achieve it. Say 'yes' more often and to things that make you feel insecure.**
- **Use these boundaries as a deterrent that keeps people at a safe distance, so they don't intrude on your happiness.**
- **Commit to consistently developing yourself and become a lifelong learner.**

Ways You Can Overcome Self-Sabotage:

- **Become Aware of your Self-Sabotage.**
- **Develop a Growth Mindset.**
- **Accept Feelings of Resistance.**
- **Start Practicing Self-Compassion.**
- **Change the Way you Talk to Yourself**
- **Practice getting Comfortable with Failure.**
- **Therapy Can Help.**

www.ingramcontent.com/pod-product-compliance
Lightning Source LLC
Chambersburg PA
CBHW062004180426
43198CB00036B/2342